A Gift For You

From:

The World Beyond:

The Mysteries Of Heaven And How To Get There

DAVE WILLIAMS

The World Beyond:
The Mysteries
Of Heaven
And How To Get There

DAVE WILLIAMS

The World Beyond:
The Mysteries Of Heaven
and How To Get There

Unless otherwise indicated, all scripture quotations are taken from the King James Version of the Bible.

Copyright ©2002 by David R. Williams

ISBN 0-938020-58-7

First Printing 2002

Published by

DECAPOLIS
PUBLISHING

Printed in the United States of America

BOOKS BY DAVE WILLIAMS

ABCs Of Success And Happiness
Aids Plague
Art Of Pacesetting Leadership
Beauty Of Holiness
Christian Job Hunter's Handbook
Desires Of Your Heart
Depression, Cave Of Torment
Genuine Prosperity, The Power To Get Wealth
Getting To Know Your Heavenly Father
Gifts That Shape Your Life And Change Your World
Grand Finale Revival
Grief And Mourning
Growing Up In Our Father's Family
Have You Heard From The Lord Lately?
How To Be A High Performance Believer
Laying On Of Hands
Lonely In The Midst Of A Crowd
Miracle Results Of Fasting
The New Life . . . The Start Of Something Wonderful
La Nueva Vida (The New Life . . . Spanish)
Pastor's Pay
Patient Determination
Road To Radical Riches
Revival Power Of Music
Secret Of Power With God
Seven Signposts On The Road To Spiritual Maturity
Slain In The Spirit — Real Or Fake?
Somebody Out There Needs You
Success Principles From The Lips Of Jesus
Supernatural Soulwinning
Thirty-six Minutes With The Pastor
Tongues And Interpretation
Understanding Spiritual Gifts
What To Do If You Miss The Rapture
World Beyond- The Mysteries Of Heaven
Your Pastor - Key To Your Personal Wealth

This book is dedicated to the memory of my flight instructor and precious friend,

William Spratt

who took his flight to "The World Beyond" in July of 2001, and to his lovely family, Lois, Jack, Ann, and Joy.

Contents

"God invites all of us to take the exciting journey to Heaven."

First Thoughts

Have you ever wondered about the world beyond this life? Heaven. What will it be like? Is it real? How long will it last? What is it made of?

Where did you learn about Heaven? Television shows? Church? A parent? A preacher? A friend?

This book is about Heaven — the world beyond — one of my favorite subjects. I want to answer some of the common questions people have about Heaven, and as a pastor, I hear many questions. Most people want to know how to get to Heaven, or if they will see their loved ones there. This book will provide answers to those and many other questions.

Do we have all the answers about Heaven? No. It remains in large part a mystery, but the Bible has not left us without answers, and in this book we will look at what we do know. Much of it will surprise you.

All of it will encourage you. And I believe that when you have finished, your life will be changed forever.

God invites all of us to take the journey to Heaven, and in this book I want us to take a look at what we know about Heaven. The Bible is our travel guide. We will also learn from the experiences of people who have been to the world beyond; whose experiences line up with Scripture. Heaven is for anyone who will have it, and I hope and pray that you will grab hold of it and never let go.

If you want assurance that you are going to Heaven right now, I invite you to turn to page 61 and begin there. The first step toward Heaven is knowing Jesus, and that chapter will show you how. Maybe you want to read a little more about Heaven before making a decision. Friend, read on and join me as we unveil the mysteries of Heaven — what it is, what it is not, why people go there and what awaits us when we arrive.

Dave Williams

Sacramento, California

Chapter One

Heaven In Our Hearts

When you think of Heaven, what pops into your mind?

Quick, capture those images. What are they? Golden harps? Fluffy clouds? Angels in white robes?

What did you feel? Boredom? Happiness? Wonder? Confusion?

What happens in Heaven? Are there businesses? Houses? Do people go shopping? Eat? Talk? Work? Play?

Who goes to Heaven? Will we see relatives there? Will it be like earth, but without things like disease and war? Or will it be a totally different kind of place?

Heaven cannot be very accurately described in human terms. Words are too humble a vehicle to convey its beauty, but I think we sometimes get a glimpse of Heaven in this life.

• We glimpse it when we look into the eyes of a child.

• We glimpse it when we fall in love.

• We glimpse it when the awe of nature seizes our hearts on a sunny mountainside.

• We glimpse it in our highest, purest moments of laughter and joy.

• We even glimpse it in our lowest moments, when hope shines through the darkness like a thin ray of light.

Are these things Heaven? No, but they are hints of Heaven, as if God were allowing His angels to serve us samples of what we can expect on the other side.

The Bible talks about the world beyond this life. It is a mystery, but a mystery with plenty of clues. In the Bible there are more than one-hundred and fifty references to Heaven. The Bible says it is a place of unimaginable joy and peace, where dreams come to life, and greater dreams are dreamt — and then lived. When we die in a right standing with God, we are carried by an angel into that place, and we feel complete fulfillment.

The Bible tells us that Heaven is as real a destination as Disneyland, the Florida Keys or New York City. It is not a place that exists only in the mind or imagination because Jesus said He was going to prepare a *place* for us — a real, solid honest-to-goodness *place*, not just some airy cloud or fuzzy consciousness. Heaven is more real than the physical world that surrounds us.

> Let not your heart be troubled: ye believe in God, believe also in me. In my Father's house are many mansions: if it were not so, I would have told you. I go to prepare a place for you. And if I go and prepare a place for you, I will come again, and receive you unto myself; that where I am, there you may be also.
>
> — John 14:1-3

Heaven is a *place* where those kinds of untouchable realities take on touchable forms, where unseen worlds of wonder spring to life.

A Tour Of Heaven

Yes, there is a world beyond this earthly life that awaits each person. Most people believe deep in their hearts that death does not mark the end of consciousness. I've read several surveys recently that showed that most Americans believe in the afterlife, and one survey conducted around the world found that three out of four people believe in Heaven.

Mary Baxter, a dear Christian woman, wrote two books called *Divine Revelation of Hell* and *Divine Revelation of Heaven* based on experiences the Lord gave her. In them she testified to being shown around Heaven and hell by an angel, then returning to her body here on earth. I don't know if you believe testimonies from the afterlife, but I do, to a certain degree. Even the Bible indicates that such experiences can be valid. I believe that many people have genuine experiences in which they go briefly to Heaven, see Jesus, perhaps get a glimpse of the Heavenly city, are reunited with loved ones, then come back to finish their tasks on this planet. Their experiences can be inspirational to us, though they cannot be used to shape our core doctrines and beliefs. They are useful and wonderful to us inasmuch as they agree with God's Word.

In Heaven, Baxter found herself outside some beautiful gates made of pearls and precious stones. An angel opened a book and when he found Mary's name the gates mysteriously opened and she walked through. Another angel began to show her around the Heavenly city— the world beyond.

She went into the Room of Records, and as far as the eye could see there were books. The book of Revelation in the Bible tells us that all of our works are written down in books in Heaven. Baxter said some of the books she saw were ordinary, others were diamond studded with silver pages full of writing that looked like it had been penned in diamond ink. In those books, everything was recorded, and the room was full of recording angels who were always writing in the books.

> And I saw the dead, small and great, stand before God; and the books were opened: and another book was opened, which is the book of life: and the dead were judged out of those things which were written in the books, according to their works.
>
> — Revelation 20:12

She was taken to a room called the Room of Tears. In Psalm 56, David wrote about God collecting David's tears in bottles as David was crying out in prayer.

> Thou tellest my wanderings: put thou my tears into thy bottle: are they not in thy book? When I cry unto thee, then shall mine enemies turn back: this I know; for God is for me.
>
> — Psalm 56:8-9

Baxter said angels would catch every tear in a bottle and label it. Then an angel would take bottles of tears that were cried on earth and put drops of tears on a large scroll, and on that scroll the liquid would become a beautiful prayer which was delivered to the throne of God.

Those who sow in tears will reap with songs of joy.

— Psalm 126:5

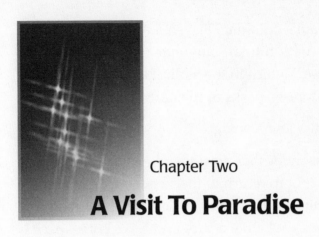

Chapter Two

A Visit To Paradise

Many people like Mary Baxter have had near-death, or "beyond and back" experiences. Ezekiel and Isaiah, two Old Testament prophets, had visions of Heaven and their descriptions of the creatures they saw are awe-inspiring.

The Apostle Paul was caught up into what he called the third Heaven as if by a high-powered magnet or irresistible force.

> I know a man in Christ who fourteen years ago was caught up to the third heaven. Whether it was in the body or out of the body I do not know — God knows. And I know that this man — whether in the body, or apart from the body, I do not know, but God knows — was caught up into paradise. He heard inexpressible things, things that man is not permitted to tell.
>
> — 2 Corinthians 12:2-4

In Paul's opinion, Heaven was too wonderful to foul up with human language. He used the word "paradise," which in the biblical language means orchards, forests, parks or meadows.

What a lovely image!

No wonder that most people who go to Heaven and are told to return to their bodies desperately resist coming back. Ultimately, in these "beyond and back" cases, whether a person stays or comes back is up to Jesus.

From that point on in his life, Paul desired to go back to Heaven. He said in a letter to believers in Philippi:

> For to me to live is Christ, and to die is gain. If I am to go on living in the body, this will mean fruitful labor for me. Yet what shall I choose? I do not know! I am torn between the two: I desire to depart and be with Christ, which is better by far; but it is more necessary for you that I remain in the body.
>
> — Philippians 1:21-24

Have you ever had one of those days that was so wonderful that it seemed like a dream? At the end of it you probably thought, as I have, "If only I could make this day go on forever." That is how Paul felt.

Snapshots Of Heaven

A man I knew of in southern California was rushed to the hospital with a heart attack. Medics worked on him, but he had been dead for several minutes. They could not resuscitate him.

The man's pastor, a Spirit-filled, Bible-believing man, came to the hospital and when the nurses tried to stop him from going in, he told them he was clergy and kept on going. Most people don't know it, but in hospitals, clergymen have more authority than even the doctors do.

Once in the room he saw the lifeless body of his parishioner. Something powerful rose up in the pastor's chest, and he pointed at the body and said, "In the Name of Jesus Christ, you come back," and continued commanding until suddenly the body moved. The doctors came in, hooked the patient up and found that he was alive.

When the parishioner came to his senses some hours later, he looked at the pastor and said, "I can't stand you."

The pastor was shocked and replied, "But I came up to pray for you."

The man said, "I know, but I departed from this old wrecked body. I was hovering over the hospital.

I could see myself laying there. I was free from pain, had perfect peace, perfect joy, and I knew I was going to be with Jesus. I went through a dark tunnel, and an angel was carrying me over to the holy city. There was a great river and meadows, and orchards. It was beautiful, and I could see the Crystal City. I knew if I could just get across that river I would be there to stay, and then I looked down and saw you pulling your car into the hospital. I saw you coming up the elevator, and the little fight you had with the nurses to get into my room. I saw you come inside and command me back, and when you did I felt my spirit leaving the glories of paradise. I knew if I could just get across that river I could stay there, but you kept commanding me back, and I kept being pulled back farther and farther away until all of a sudden the pain was back and now here I am."

That parishioner, a real person, went on to live a long and fruitful life.

Heaven's Annex

I believe the earth was created to be sort of an annex of Heaven. In the beginning God placed man in a beautiful paradise on earth, the Garden of Eden, but when man sinned, earth was cut off from Heaven.

Fortunately, that is not the end of the story. The Bible says one day there is going to be a renovated earth and renovated heavens, and the two once again are going to be one, joined together by a city called "New Jerusalem." The Bible talks about this new city that will come down out of Heaven.

> ...you have come to Mount Zion, to the city of the living God, the heavenly Jerusalem, and to thousands of angels in joyful assembly.
>
> — Hebrews 12:22 (NLT)

Jesus is preparing a place for His followers in that city right now. He said:

> In my Father's house are many mansions: *if it were not so*, I would have told you. I go to prepare a place for you. And if I go and prepare a place for you, I will come again, and receive you unto myself; that where I am, *there* ye may be also.
>
> — John 14:2,3

Many, even before Jesus' time, looked forward to that promised place.

> By faith Abraham, when called to go to a place he would later receive as his inheritance, obeyed and went, even though he did not know where he was going. By faith he made his home in the promised land like a stranger in a foreign country; he lived in tents, as did Isaac and Jacob, who were heirs with him of the same promise. For he was looking forward to the city with foundations, whose architect and builder is God.
>
> — Hebrews 11:8-10

Verse 16 says:

> Instead, they were longing for a better country — a heavenly one. Therefore God is not ashamed to be called their God, for he has prepared a city for them.

— Hebrews 11:16

Every person has a longing in his or her heart to be a citizen of that coming city.

• We are disquieted by life on earth, and we may not know why.

• We wonder why we feel alienated from the world we live in, and even from those we love.

• Our deepest souls cry out for the place God is creating for us — a perfect place in the world beyond.

The Heavenly City

The Bible tells us some things about that city we will one day call home. It is in Heaven now and will come to earth in the course of the end times, a period after Jesus comes back for His followers. It is a cube-shaped city with a skyline, a throne, a river, vegetation, business, and some sort of monetary system (Jesus instructed us to lay up for ourselves treasures in Heaven, therefore it must be possible to have some kind of treasure there).

Lay not up for yourselves treasures upon earth, where moth and rust doth corrupt, and where thieves break through and steal: But lay up for yourselves treasures in heaven, where neither moth nor rust doth corrupt, and where thieves do not break through nor steal: For where your treasure is, there will your heart be also.

— Matthew 6:19-21

John saw the city in his vision:

I saw the Holy City, the new Jerusalem, coming down out of heaven from God, prepared as a bride beautifully dressed for her husband. And I heard a loud voice from the throne saying, 'Now the dwelling of God is with men, and he will live with them. They will be his people, and God himself will be with them, and be their God. He will wipe every tear from their eyes. There will be no more death or mourning or crying or pain, for the old order of things has passed away'

— Revelation 21:2-4

And he carried me away in the Spirit to a mountain great and high, and showed me the Holy City, Jerusalem, coming down out of heaven from God. It shone with the glory of God, and its brilliance was like that of a very precious jewel, like jasper, clear as crystal. It had a great, high wall with twelve gates, and with twelve angels at the gates. On the gates were written the names of the twelve tribes of Israel.

— Revelation 21:10-12

The city was laid out like a square, as long as it was wide. He measured the city with a rod and found it to be 12,000 stadia [about 1,400

miles] in length, and as wide and high as it is
long.

— Revelation 21:16

The wall was made of jasper, and the city of
pure gold, as pure as glass. The foundations of
the wall of the city were decorated with every
kind of precious stone

— Revelation 21:18,19a

Then the angel showed me the river of the water of life, as clear as crystal, flowing from the
throne of God and of the Lamb down the
middle of the great street of the city. On each
side of the river stood the tree of life, bearing
twelve crops of fruit, yielding its fruit every
month. And the leaves of the tree are for the
healing of the nations.

— Revelation 22:1,2

That is the place we will live with Jesus. A city
that is cube-shaped — 1,400 miles wide, long and
high — and teeming with wealth and activity.

What else do we know about the world beyond?
How do we describe it? What does the Bible tell us,
in concrete terms, about what we can expect? In the
next chapter, we'll take a look at some astounding
and wonderful facts about Heaven— the world beyond.

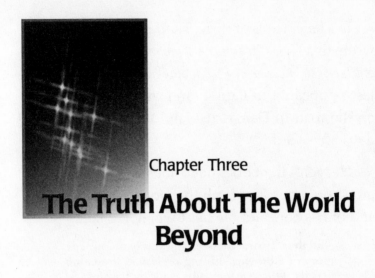

Chapter Three

The Truth About The World Beyond

Let's look at some of the wonderful facts the Bible tells us about Heaven.

■ *Wonderful Fact Number One: Heaven is full of light.*

Have you ever stared straight into a spotlight, or seen lightning flash close by? Those are nothing compared to the brightness of Heaven.

Heaven's light is so intense and powerful that mortals, in their physical bodies, cannot even get near it. Night never falls in Heaven. There is no dusk, no sunrise, no midnight hour.

> **The sun will not beat upon them, nor any scorching heat.**
>
> — **Revelation 7:16b**

In a letter to his protege, Timothy, the Apostle Paul wrote that God *"lives in unapproachable light, whom no one has seen or can see,"* (1 Timothy 6:16b). Indeed, when Jesus appeared to Paul in an extremely bright light on the road to Damascus, Paul was blind for three days afterward.

Heaven's light does not come from the sun or the moon or lamps, but from the glory of God Himself, and of His Son, and the light will never fade.

> And the city did not need the sun or moon. The glory of God was shining on it, and the Lamb was its light. Nations will walk by the light of that city, and kings will bring their riches there. Its gates are always open during the day and night never comes.
>
> — Revelation 21:23-25 (CEV)

■ *Wonderful Fact Number Two: Nobody is hungry or thirsty in Heaven.*

There are no famines in Heaven. No pictures of starving children in foreign countries. There is no drought, no crop failure, no empty pantries. You will never hear a stomach growl or a baby cry because of lack of food.

> They shall hunger no more, neither thirst any more ... for the Lamb that is in the midst of the throne shall be their shepherd, and shall guide them unto fountains of waters of life.
>
> — Revelation 7:16, 17 (ASB)

And here's a delightful benefit: you do not have to count calories, fat grams or carbohydrates because the food in Heaven will not make you fat! There is going to be a feast called the marriage supper of the Lamb, and you can eat as much as you want.

■ *Wonderful Fact Number Three: There will be animals and creatures in Heaven.*

The Bible talks about creatures worshipping before the throne of God, and goes on to even describe six horses. Indeed, Jesus Himself will ride on a horse.

> I looked and saw that heaven was open, and a white horse was there. Its rider was called Faithful and True, and he is always fair when he judges or goes to war.
>
> — Revelation 19:11 (CEV)

Many years ago I witnessed a man callously throw a small kitten out of his car as he sped by the front of my house. The little buff-colored kitten limped up to my door and began to purr. She seemed afraid, lonely, hurt, and hungry, so I fed her some tuna fish, prepared her a dish of milk, and she decided she would stay.

For nineteen years Bobo was my loyal friend, and not long ago she died in my arms. She was one-hundred and thirty-three in cat years.

I do not know if there will be cats in Heaven — I hope so. I want to see Bobo again!

■ *Wonderful Fact Number Four: Nobody cries in Heaven.*

You will never see someone break down and sob in Heaven. There are no tear ducts, no quivering lower lips, no hankies and no swollen, red eyes, because:

> God shall wipe away every tear from their eyes.
>
> — **Revelation 7:17 (ASB)**

■ *Wonderful Fact Number Five: There is no sorrow, mourning or pain.*

No one will be depressed anymore. There will be no broken hearts, broken lives, broken promises. There will be no prescription drugs, no pharmacies, no antidepressants, no aspirin. There will be no broken legs, car accidents, hospitals, emergency rooms, sicknesses, aches or bruises.

> There will be no more death or mourning or crying or pain, for the old order of things has passed away.
>
> — **Revelation 21:4**

■ *Wonderful Fact Number Six: We will have perfect love for our mates.*

Like it or not, people do not get married in Heaven. There are no engagement rings, marriage certificates, wedding dresses, wedding cakes, honeymoons, receptions, gifts or groomsmen. There are no fathers-in-law, mothers-in-law, family squabbles, children or wedding anniversaries. There is no divorce, no blended families, no stepchildren, no second husbands or ex-wives. Jesus said:

> **For in the resurrection they neither marry, nor are given in marriage, but are as the angels of God in heaven.**
>
> — Matthew 22:30

For some of us, Heaven will not be Heaven without our mates, but we can take comfort in the fact that God has prepared a more perfect kind of love for us there. While marriage was created for earth, we will discover wonderful new types of relationships in Heaven. God would not take away marriage unless He intended to replace it with something better.

■ *Wonderful Fact Number Seven: There is no death.*

This is one of the best things about Heaven: there are no hearses, no funeral homes, no caskets, no cemetery plots. There are no life insurance policies, death taxes, last wills and testaments or earthly inheritances. No one is embalmed, cremated or buried. No one's ashes are ever cast into the sea. There are no grave robbers, headstones or mausoleums. Jesus said:

> Neither can they die any more: for they are equal unto the angels; and are the children of God, being the children of the resurrection.

> — Luke 20:36

> ... and there shall be no more death ...

> — Revelation 21:4

■ *Wonderful Fact Number Eight: Heaven is a place of rest.*

We will not strive or worry there. We will not concern ourselves with pay raises, promotions or Christmas bonuses. There will be no office politics, no firings, no "golden handshakes."

> ... that they may rest from their labours; and their works do follow them.

> — Revelation 14:13

■ *Wonderful Fact Number Nine: There is great rejoicing in Heaven.*

Jesus said:

> ... there is joy in the presence of the angels of God over one sinner that repenteth.

> — Luke 15:10

■ *Wonderful Fact Number Ten: There is magnificent music in Heaven.*

In fact, the Bible says there will be silence in Heaven for only about thirty minutes.

> And when he had opened the seventh seal, there was silence in heaven about the space of half an hour.
>
> — Revelation 8:1

After that, the concert will begin, and will go on forever. Heaven will have the biggest gospel choir imaginable — millions of tenors, hundreds of millions of altos, sopranos and basses.

> And they sung as it were a new song before the throne ...
>
> — Revelation 14:3

> Then I looked and heard the voice of many angels, numbering thousands upon thousands, and ten thousand times ten thousand. They encircled the throne and the living creatures and the elders. In a loud voice they sang: 'Worthy is the Lamb, who was slain, to receive power and wealth and wisdom and strength and honor and glory and praise!' Then I heard every creature in heaven and on earth and under the earth and on the sea, and all that is in them, singing: 'To Him who sits on the throne and to the Lamb be praise and honor and glory and power for ever and ever!'
>
> — Revelation 5:11-13

■ *Wonderful Fact Number Eleven: Heaven is a place of absolute perfection.*

It is a place of glory, honor and incorruption (Romans 2:7). Wickedness will not be allowed there (Ephesians 5:5). There will be no disasters. No smog. No radiation. No taxes. No mildew. No weeds. No jumper cables. No flat tires. No tow trucks. No spare tires. No mosquitoes. No flies. No snakes. No termites. No computer crashes. No cover-ups. No bills. No terrorists. No malignant, vulgar devil.

Only those who have been cleansed by the blood of Jesus will be permitted inside the gate (Revelation 21:27 and 22:14, 15).

Learning To Love

Dr. Collette was a medical missionary in the Amazon jungle for forty-eight years. Collette had witnessed some of the most marvelous miracles that anybody could ever see. He saw people with no eyes in their sockets receive new eyeballs. He saw other creative miracles too, but none of it seemed to fulfill him. It is possible to see the miracles of God and still not be satisfied.

Collette wanted one thing: to see the glory of God. Nothing else would touch his heart, so for nine years he prayed, "God, I want to see Your glory."

When he was eighty-one years old, attending a prayer meeting in the Amazon forest one night, a burst of power hit the place where they had gathered. The glory of God came down and everybody in that meeting passed out. When they woke up they found Collette dead. Somehow, it seemed that the glory of God had killed him. In that particular tribe the custom was to pack a dead person's head with mud and leave them for several days, which they did.

Dr. Collette, who later came back to life, said that he remembered hovering over his body, looking down and thinking, "What a pitiful sight that is." He had no desire to return to his body. He felt no fear or dread, but total peace. Then a strange force began to pull him upward. He could not stay there and look at his dead body any longer. He recognized the presence of two angels, one his guardian angel, the other a transport angel, and he knew at last he was going to see the glory of God.

Beyond The Stars

The angels began to carry him beyond the stars, out of our solar system at what seemed like a million miles a minute. In the distance he could see Heaven. It was as if all the stars had faces and were singing and pointing to the glory of God. As he got closer he could feel Heaven's gravity. The stars, the trees, the vegetation, everything was singing, "Holy, holy, holy," and there was great lightning and thunder.

He saw the gates of Heaven studded with giant pearls, covered with beautiful engravings, and as he arrived the gates opened and he went through. He noticed that everyone was clothed in glorious, brilliant light. He could see for miles and was dumbstruck by the magnificence of Heaven.

He saw and was allowed to speak with Abraham, the patriarch from the book of Genesis. Abraham has been there for five thousand years or so. Collette asked, "Abraham, how long have you been here?" and Abraham said, "I guess it has been about a day now." When you are in eternity, there is no way of measuring time.

Collette asked to see the mansion the Lord was preparing for him, and the angel took him there. The mansion looked like it was made out of golden boards and diamond nails. They went into a large living room which had no furniture. The angel said, "Sit down." Collette did, and a beautiful, comfortable chair appeared.

Then he had a wonderful and happy reunion with his mother. But the best part was meeting Jesus. The thing he noticed most was that the scars were still in His hands and feet. The only evidence that sin ever existed is in the scars in Jesus' body that He will carry throughout eternity to remind us how we are privileged to live in that beautiful paradise.

Dr. Collette was taken to the throne of God, which seemed to be miles long. In front of the throne was a sea of glass, and he saw hundreds of thousands of people dancing and singing and praising God.

After five-and-a-half earth days Jesus made Dr. Collette go back to earth to complete his task, and to tell people that Jesus is coming soon. The biggest lesson Collette took away from the experience was that he should love people on earth the same way he was loved in Heaven.

"Heaven has its own twenty-four-hour biography channel."

Chapter Four

Your Biography

Dr. Collette had an amazing experience of Heaven, but most of us have to rely solely on the Word of God.

There are other surprising facts that we know for certain about Heaven.

Your Biography Is Being Written In Heaven

The Bible talks about the Book of Life, which bears the names of all who will be permitted to enter Heaven. Paul wrote:

> ... help those women which laboured with me in the gospel, with Clement also, and with other my fellowlabourers, whose names are in the book of life.
>
> — Philippians 4:3

Jesus said:

> He who overcomes will, like them, be dressed in white. I will never blot out his name from

the book of life, but will acknowledge his
name before my Father and his angels.

— Revelation 3:5

There is not only the Book of Life, which says who
belongs to God's family, there are other books that
record everything we do, as Mary K. Baxter saw. The
Apostle John had a vision, recounted in the book of
Revelation, and he saw books of record in Heaven.

And I saw the dead, the great and the small,
standing before the throne; and books were
opened: and another book was opened, which
is the book of life: and the dead were judged
out of the things which were written in the
books, according to their works. And the sea
gave up the dead that were in it; and death and
Hades gave up the dead that were in them: and
they were judged every man according to their
works. And death and Hades were cast into the
lake of fire. This is the second death, even the
lake of fire. And if any was not found written
in the book of life, he was cast into the lake of
fire.

— Revelation 20:12-15 (ASB)

For better or worse, Heaven has its own twenty-
four-hour biography channel, and one day we will
be judged by whatever is found on the videotape of
our lives.

Jesus said:

But I tell you that men will have to give account on the day of judgment for every care-

less word they have spoken. For by your words you will be acquitted, and by your words you will be condemned.

— Matthew 12:36, 37

We Will Recognize People In Heaven

We will see people we know in Heaven and rejoice with them. We will even recognize people we have not met in person. Peter, James and John were with Jesus when He was transfigured, and they caught a glimpse of Him in His glory. There appeared with Him Moses and Elijah, and the disciples instantly recognized who they were even though they had never met them. In Heaven there is instant recognition and knowledge of people.

Jesus told the parable of the rich man and Lazarus. The rich man died and went to hell, and Lazarus, a poor beggar, died and went to Heaven. In the afterlife they could see and recognize each other across a great chasm, and they even had a conversation (Luke 16:19-26).

King David of the Old Testament lost a son because of his adulterous affair and the murder he committed trying to cover it up. After mourning for the child, David said, "Can I bring him back again? I shall go to him, but he will not return to me" (1 Samuel 12:23, ASB). In other words, David's son immediately went into paradise and David said he would one day be with his son in Heaven.

Heaven Is God's Dwelling Place

It is where He resides in holy splendor greater than you or I can currently imagine. Moses prayed:

> Look down from heaven, your holy dwelling place, and bless your people Israel.
>
> — Deuteronomy 26:15

In the New Testament it was said:

> The heaven is my throne, And the earth the footstool of my feet: What manner of house will ye build Me?' saith the Lord: 'Or what is the place of My rest? Did not my hand make all these things?
>
> — Acts 7:49, 50 (ASB)

No building on earth can contain God. He is beyond time and space. Not even the whole physical universe, millions of light years across, could provide enough room for Him. But Heaven is His abode, His throne, a limitless place where God lives.

God's Family Lives With Him In Heaven

Does God have family? Yes! He even invites us to call Him our Heavenly Father. All those who accept Jesus Christ as Lord belong to God's family. There is no secret handshake or ritual, no special categories. The invitation to join is open to anyone.

Jesus was called the firstborn of many brothers (Romans 8:29). In the Gospels, He made a distinction between Heavenly relatives and earthly relatives when He said:

> Who is my mother? and who are my brethren? And he stretched forth his hand towards his disciples, and said, Behold, my mother and my brethren! For whosoever shall do the will of my Father who is in heaven, he is my brother, and sister, and mother.

> — Matthew 12:48-50 (ASB)

For the believer, true family is known by spiritual condition, not by blood. This is not to say that physical family is meaningless. God places great emphasis on the care and closeness of our biological families. But ultimately, Heaven will reveal that our brothers and sisters are those who have been born again through Christ. Paul said:

> But our citizenship is in heaven. And we eagerly await a Savior from there, the Lord Jesus Christ.

> — Philippians 3:20

And:

> Consequently, you are no longer foreigners and aliens, but fellow citizens with God's people and members of God's household, built on the foundation of the apostles and prophets, with Christ Jesus himself as the chief cornerstone.

> — Ephesians 2:19, 20

How do we know who is in God's family? In the end, only God knows the true condition of a man or woman's heart.

> The Lord knows those who are his.

> — 2 Timothy 2:19 (ASB)

People Who Do Not Go To Heaven Will Be Forgotten

How can we enjoy Heaven if someone we love is in hell?

God said through the prophet Isaiah, "For, behold, I create new Heavens and a new earth; and the former things shall not be remembered, nor come into mind," (Isaiah 65:17,ASB). Those *not* in Heaven will be erased from memory.

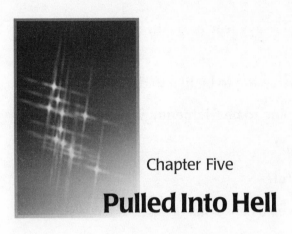

Chapter Five

Pulled Into Hell

The only unfortunate thing about Heaven is that not everybody will go there. Nothing in the Bible leads us to believe that mankind will experience a wholesale transition from earth to Heaven, as many people believe will happen.

Every person falls into one of two categories: either we are Heaven bound, or we are hell bound. Jesus made it simple. There are saved and unsaved people. Not kinda-sorta saved. Not super-duper saved. Just saved and unsaved. And what you are determines where you go.

I have heard numerous testimonies over the years about people who claimed to have had Paul-like experiences and been caught up into Heaven. One of the hallmarks of these experiences is that when people come back to their bodies, they no longer fear death.

Hebrews 2:15 says fear of death binds and enslaves people.

What is it going to be like to die?

• Is it going to be frightening?

• Painful?

• Peaceful?

• Will we be conscious of what is happening?

Each of us wants the answers to these questions. The Bible says that those who are in Christ have already passed over from death to life. Paul said that death is swallowed up in victory. Those of us who know Jesus should not fear death, even if we have not been to Heaven and back.

When the famous preacher D.L. Moody was in his last few moments of life, he lay on his bed with his eyes closed. All of a sudden he said, "Earth is receding and the Heavens are opening." Somebody in the room remarked that he must be dreaming. Moody looked up and said, "This is no dream. This is the day I have been waiting for. It is my coronation day— good-bye," and he left for Heaven—the world beyond.

A precious man who started a school for people who wanted to preach the Gospel never feared death.

One evening he was on stage during a meeting, and all of his students were before him. He started waving at them. Then he bowed his head and died. No fear, no pain, he just slipped into beautiful paradise. He simply left this world.

One famous preacher was dying. He looked up, smiled and said, "It is beautiful, it is beautiful, good-bye."

When one of the world's most famous revivalists, John Wesley, was in his last few moments of life, he looked up and shouted, "I will praise Him, I will praise Him," then he looked around the room and said, "Farewell, everybody," and away he went.

The Tunnel Of Light

The joke goes like this: There was a man from Michigan who was going down to Florida. He took his laptop computer with him and decided to e-mail his wife. He plugged in the computer and sent her a note, but mailed it to the wrong e-mail address. It went instead to a widow of a minister who had died that week. When she got the e-mail, she fainted. It read, "I had a wonderful trip, but it sure is hot down here."

The greatest tragedy is when people die who do not know Jesus Christ. Because only Jesus can give us access to Heaven. There is no other way. Period.

> Jesus said unto him, I am the way, the truth,
> and the life: no man cometh to the Father, but
> by me.
>
> — John 14:6

When a Christian dies, the Bible tells us he or she is transported to Heaven by an angel (Luke 16:22). But when someone dies without accepting Christ, they are pulled down into hell.

I read about the dying moments of Desi Arnaz, who played Ricky Ricardo on television's "I Love Lucy." His daughter was there with him, and apparently she had been studying some of the new age philosophies. She kept saying to him, "Daddy, follow the light." Arnaz died trying to follow the light.

The problem is, as we are told in the Scriptures, Satan comes disguised as an angel of light.

> . . . for Satan himself is transformed into an
> angel of light.
>
> — 2 Corinthians 11:14

A number of believers who have gone to Heaven and come back say that they traveled through a long, dark tunnel with a light at the end of it, and at that light is a fork in the road. Waiting there is a transport angel for Christians, but there is a deceiving angel for unbelievers.

That fork in the road is a separation place.

Once people get through that dark tunnel — no matter how much peace and love they feel going through it — a separation takes place. Those who have known and followed Christ are transported by an angel to the holy city. The others are immediately drawn down to the regions of the damned, where they will be incarcerated along with other lost souls, to await the final judgment the Bible warns us about.

> And the devil that deceived them was cast into the lake of fire and brimstone, where the beast and false prophet are, and shall be tormented day and night for ever and ever. And I saw a great white throne, and him who sat on it, from whose face the earth and heaven fled away; and there was found no place for them. And I saw the dead, small and great, stand before God; and the books were opened: and another book was opened, which is the book of life: and the dead were judged out of those things which were written in the books, according to their works. And the sea gave up the dead which were in it; and death and hell delivered up the dead which were in them: and they were judged every man according to their works. And death and hell were cast into the lake of fire. This is the second death. And whosoever was not found written in the book of life was cast into the lake of fire.
>
> — Revelation 20:10-15

I went to the hospital one time to see an elderly woman whom the nurses said was unconscious. She had gone into a coma. I asked if I could try to speak to her, so I knelt down by her bed and whispered in her ear, "Agnes, I am here to pray with you. Do you understand me?" Her eyes opened and on her face was a horrified look. I asked, "Do you want me to pray with you to receive Jesus as your Savior so you can go to Heaven?" She nodded her head with a look of desperation.

I grabbed her hand and said, "Even if you can't talk, the Bible says the Holy Spirit will help you with groans which cannot be uttered. Squeeze my hand if you are praying this with me in your heart. Pray this: 'Jesus, I believe you are the Son of God.'" I felt a little squeeze on my hand. "'I believe you died on the cross for my sins.'" I felt another little squeeze. "'I believe you were raised from the dead. Forgive me of all my sins, and give me a home in Heaven. Amen.'" She squeezed again, and I looked into her eyes and they began to twinkle. A tear came out of one of her eyes, she smiled and then left for Heaven.

Her final destination had just changed.

The Garbage Dump of the Universe

The Bible talks quite a lot about hell, a place shrouded in mystery. We know it is a place of regret and sorrow, darkness and blackness, separation from God. We know it is a place of no hope whatsoever, and we know that it is permanent -- forever.

There are plenty of false beliefs circulating about hell.

• Some say hell does not exist.

• Some say hell is only for murderers and heartless sinners.

• Some say hell is here and now.

Many people believe that every sinner who ever lived will go to hell, but that would mean every person ever born, except Jesus, would go there because all of us either are now or were sinners at one time.

People do not go to hell because they sin. They go to hell because they refuse the remedy for sin. The Bible says all have sinned and we are all doomed without Jesus Christ.

All those who refuse to receive Christ will be thrown into hell, a place Jesus called "Gehena." Gehena was a garbage dump outside of Jerusalem, and it was constantly smoldering. Jesus used the word to describe the final destination of those who did not believe in Him, meaning that the best way to describe hell is as the garbage dump of the universe.

Hell is the unseen world of departed, unredeemed spirits. The Bible tells us where hell is.

• It is in the nether (lower) parts of the earth (Ezekiel 31:14-18, and 32:24, Psalms 63:9, Ephesians 4:9).

• It is in the heart of the earth (Matthew 12:40).

The Bible says that there is a force that pulls people into hell after they die without Christ. Ezekiel 31:15-17 talks about a casting down, like an upside-down ejection seat that propels you into hell.

> Let death seize my enemies by surprise; let the grave swallow them alive, for evil makes its home within them.
>
> — Psalm 55:15 (NLT)

David said hell swallowed people. In Jesus' parable of the rich man and Lazarus, there was no angel carrying the rich man into hell. The rich man was simply pulled down as if by suction.

Some of the children of Israel who had done evil were literally swallowed up by the ground.

> He [Moses] had hardly finished speaking when the ground suddenly split open beneath them. The earth opened up and swallowed the men, along with their households and the followers who were standing with them, and everything they owned. So they went down alive into the grave, along with their belongings. The earth closed over them and they vanished.
>
> — Numbers 16:31-33 (NLT)

I believe that is a picture of what happens spiritually when people go to hell. They go suddenly, quickly and without recourse or remedy.

The Pain Of Hell

I read true accounts from a doctor who said that he had resuscitated just as many people who were on their way to hell as to Heaven. He said they came back screaming, with their veins bulging out of their neck and their eye balls popping out. That doctor is now a Christian minister who, prior to his conversion, died and went to hell himself and was resuscitated. He testified that when his spirit left his body, he went through a tunnel he thought would lead him to Heaven. He saw a bright white light, and suddenly a great suctioning force grabbed hold of him and down he went. He could see the glow of hell as he approached the center of the earth, and he screamed in terror. He saw hideous creatures there grabbing for him, but then was resuscitated and his spirit came back into his body.

What is it like in hell? Jesus said in Luke 16 that it is a place of torment, anguish and foul-smelling, smoldering fire. The rich man in Jesus' story had spent his life accumulating wealth, not helping others. He was the kind of guy who said things like, "If Lazarus would get a job, he would not be poor. If he had health insurance, he would not have to have the dogs lick those sores." He always had an excuse for not helping somebody.

When the rich man was sucked down to hell, he left his clothes, his comfort, his ease behind. But he did take something to hell with him.

His senses.

In hell, people have the power to feel. Everyone who dies will be given a resurrected, indestructible body, whether they go to Heaven or hell.

> In hell, where he was in torment, he looked up and saw Abraham far away, with Lazarus by his side. So he called to him, 'Father Abraham, have pity on me and send Lazarus to dip the tip of his finger in water and cool my tongue, because I am in agony in this fire.
>
> — Luke 16:23, 24 (NIV)

The rich man had the power to see, to speak, to remember, to hear, to feel sensations on his skin, to have thirst in his mouth and hunger in his belly. All of his natural functions and drives were still there, but none of them would ever be satisfied.

He did not believe in hell — until he got there. He had five brothers he wanted to warn so they would not end up in torment as well, but prayers from hell do not get answered. There is no mercy in hell, no grace. It is a place beyond the shadow of the Cross.

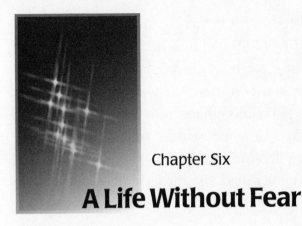

Chapter Six

A Life Without Fear

Death always comes too soon. Nobody is ever ready. A knock at the door, a ring of the phone, and it has arrived. You see it every day in the pages of the newspaper.

People are constantly being ushered into Heaven or sucked into hell. I had a friend who was killed instantly by a drunk driver. I read about an excellent swimmer who drowned in a lake near my home. I knew a man who recently suffered a heart attack and died a few hours later. Death happens every day. It will come to each one of us. When it does, there will be no second chance.

Can We Be Sure?

How can we be sure that we are going to Heaven?

I used to have a recurring dream. In it, I would die. Then I would travel through space and arrive at a big waiting room where people were being held before they went on trial. As I waited, I wondered if I had been good enough to make it into Heaven, or if I would be condemned to hell. I was tortured by fear. Each time I dreamed this, I would wake up just before I was to be called into the judgment hall to learn my fate.

Everyone wonders what will happen after they die. Some pretend they do not care and say things like, "When I die, I hope I go to hell because that is where all my friends will be." They do not understand that even if their friends are there, they will be transformed by their horrible suffering into unrecognizable beings.

Others try to comfort themselves with the belief that if the good they did in their lives outweighs the bad, they will end up in Heaven. It is amazing to hear the variety of answers you get when you ask someone how to get to Heaven.

Where Will You Go?

Do you know where you will spend eternity?

Your answer to one simple question holds the key to your salvation and your final destiny after death.

That question is this: "If you were to die right now, and you found yourself standing before God, what would you say when He asks you, 'Why should I let you into Heaven?'" Think about that question carefully. How would you answer God?

• "Well, I have been a good person. I have given to charities and lived an honest life."

• "I was a member of the church and went every Sunday morning."

• "I have always tried to serve the Lord."

• "I have tried to live my life by the ten commandments."

• "I studied my Bible."

• "God is good. I know He would not condemn me to hell."

In reality, none of these answers is sufficient. Yes, it is great to be involved in a good church, to study the Bible. But, if that is the only justification you have to offer God for your entry into Heaven, it will not be enough. There is only one right answer.

"I trusted in Jesus Christ, the Son of God, gave him my heart and confessed Him as my Lord."

Jesus told us that only those who are "born again" will see the Kingdom of God.

> In reply Jesus declared, 'I tell you the truth, no one can see the kingdom of God unless he is born again.'
>
> — John 3:3

> Jesus answered, 'I am the way and the truth and the life. No one comes to the Father except through Me.'
>
> — John 14:6

Earning Heaven?

I visited a church one time, and there was a lady playing the piano. She had her hair all up in a bun. The pastor asked for people to give testimonies, and she stood up and said, "Fifty years ago I accepted Jesus as my Savior. Someday I am going to be leaving this life, and I just hope I have done enough to please Him so I will be able to get into Heaven."

How tragic that a person who received Jesus is worried about whether she has done enough to make it to Heaven! What a profound misunderstanding of the Gospel, which offers grace apart from our power to earn it. We could never be good enough to deserve Heaven! Only the goodness of God makes it possible to go there, and that goodness is embodied in Jesus Christ.

Do you have the assurance that you are going to Heaven? Or do thoughts of the world beyond frighten you? Read on to see how you can be rid of that fear forever.

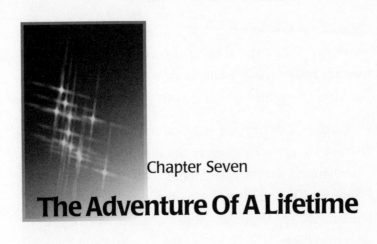

Chapter Seven

The Adventure Of A Lifetime

Life is about choosing your own adventure. You can choose the world's adventure, or you can choose God's adventure. The world's adventure is like a roller coaster that ends up going off track. It looks appealing when you are waiting to ride, and the first couple of turns and drops are a blast. But then, as you plummet down a steep curve you see that the track ends suddenly, and there in a pile are dozens of other cars that have already been wrecked.

The world has an adventure, yes. But the price is steep.

God's Great Adventure

Then there is God's adventure. It sometimes looks a little plain, and may not seem adventurous at all. Many people may avoid God's adventure because it doesn't appear to offer the immediate thrills of the other rides. But those who choose it find an adventure no roller coaster can match — true adventure, the kind the world can only envy.

God is looking for true adventurers to be with Him in Heaven. Heaven is the eternal destination of every man, woman and child who follows Jesus. There will be adventures in the world beyond that we cannot speak about here because words cannot describe them.

Don't You Want To Be Part Of Them?

I do. And I want you to be there, too. I know that you would be a great companion on God's adventure.

Your Heavenly visit can begin right now. No, I am not talking about dying, I am talking about living. Jesus said that for the believer there is no death. You will never die! Oh sure, your body will fall to the ground one day and not get up. People will lay you in a casket lined with fabric, drive in procession to the cemetery and put your body in the ground; but by that time you will be long gone, into a glorious place with no sickness, no worry, no tears. You will be with the Lord.

Will you go, or will you not? Believe it or not, the choice is yours. You do not have to measure up to a standard, or try to be a good person. You can come as you are.

Some may say, "If God wanted to save me, He would come down and save me. I wouldn't have to say anything." If that is your attitude, you will die and go to hell. For a gift to be a gift, it has to be received. Forgiveness is a gift that only becomes effective when you reach out and grab it.

In The Beginning

Back when God created Adam and Eve, men and women had perfect fellowship with God. Can you imagine walking with God through the garden, having little chats under a palm tree?

People work all their lives to get what Adam and Eve already had, a tropical paradise with trees and fruits and tame animals. God said, "Adam, give names to all the animals. Work the garden and enjoy it. Enjoy the fellowship that we have with one another. You can eat anything, have fun, do anything, except one thing. I have one moral law: Do not eat of that tree over there. That is the tree of the knowledge of good and evil."

One day a voice of disharmony and discord came into the garden and made some tempting suggestions. "Eve, Adam, God is a liar. He doesn't want you to eat of that tree because you will become like Him if you do. He is cheating you."

Every time any one of us has violated one of God's moral laws, it is because we have listened to the voice of disharmony, and the tragedy that resulted from Adam and Eve listening to that voice of disharmony was the spiritual death that entered the human race. Fellowship was broken with the Holy God. No more could God walk in the cool of the day with His beloved creation because now sin had spotted their souls.

There is nothing we can do about it because we inherited sin and, of course we've all sinned by choice as men. That's why we need a Savior. The Bible says that if you have violated only one law, you have violated them all because God's laws are like a chain. You can break just one link, and when you do the whole thing falls apart. Have you ever told a lie? You've sinned. Ever gossiped? You've sinned. Ever failed to honor God's holy day? You've sinned.

Why Me?

Why do we come to the Savior? Why do you need Jesus Christ? Not because He will keep you out of trouble. Not because He will give you peace. He will do these things, but the real reason you need Him is because you are a law breaker, just like me and everybody else on the planet. You have violated God's holy commandments. All have sinned and come short of the glory of God.

> **For all have sinned, and come short of the glory of God.**
>
> — **Romans 3:23**

God said, *The only way to get these people out of the mess they are in is to invade the human race, become one of them, and win them back from the devil's control.* So the Holy Spirit overshadowed this little virgin, and she conceived a Child by the Holy Spirit, and they called Him Jesus. He lived a sinless life. He went about doing good and healing all that were oppressed of the devil.

> **How God anointed Jesus of Nazareth with the Holy Ghost and with power: who went about doing good, and healing all that were oppressed of the devil; for God was with him.**
>
> — **Acts 10:38**

Some people, especially the religious ones, did not like God's Son. They blasphemed and ridiculed Him. They said He was:

- demon-possessed,

- a glutton,

- a drunkard,

- a friend of sinners and prostitutes.

Finally, in collaboration with the Roman government, they had Him hung on a cross of execution. They put a crown of thorns on His head, drove nails in His hands and feet and jabbed a spear in His side. Slowly and agonizingly this God who invaded the human race died a torturously painful death. And the Bible says He took our sins on His body that day so we would not have to pay the price.

That means that even though we all have sinned and come short of the glory of God, God made a provision for us to one day have a home in Heaven.

> For the wages of sin is death; but the gift of God is eternal life through Jesus Christ our Lord.
>
> — Romans 6:23

Jesus said:

> In my Father's house are many mansions: if it were not so, I would have told you. I go prepare a place for you. And if I go and prepare a place for you, I will come again, and receive you unto myself; that where I am, there ye may be also.
>
> — John 14:2-3

He died on that cross. Three days later, death could not hold Him in the grave any longer, and the power of the Holy Spirit came upon that dead body in that tomb outside of Jerusalem, the sparks began to fly, the energy was turned up, the power began to surge through the body, and out of that grave walked Jesus! Alive!

Heaven Is Yours

He still does miracles, and He has a miracle in store for you, too. Have you ever wished you could start your life all over again? Jesus, God's Son, made a way for you to experience a brand new life. You *can* start over, regardless of how many bad things you have done or how messed up you may feel right now.

The Apostle Paul put it this way:

> For there is one God, and one mediator between God and men, the man Christ Jesus.
>
> — 1 Timothy 2:5

> Therefore, if anyone is in Christ, he is a new creation; the old has gone, the new has come!
>
> — 2 Corinthians 5:17

Can you believe it? Heaven is yours with no strings attached. God's forgiveness, acceptance, and power are available to you right now, just for the asking. God has done His part to give you a new life and someday a home in Heaven. Now it is up to you.

1. *Come to Jesus as you are (Romans 3:23).*

2. *Admit your helplessness to save yourself (Romans 6:23; Luke 18:13).*

3. *Ask Jesus to be your Savior and to give you a new start (2 Corinthians 5:17).*

4. *Confess with your mouth that He is your Lord (Romans 10:9).*

5. *By faith, receive Christ into your life (John 1:11-12).*

The burden of sin will quickly be rolled away if you do these things. God is standing by you right now to hear you pray. He is ready to send Jesus into your life and is calling the angels together for a celebration in Heaven — a celebration over you! Jesus said:

> I tell you that in the same way there will be more rejoicing in heaven over one sinner who repents than over ninety-nine righteous persons who do not need to repent.
>
> — Luke 15:7

Perhaps you are planning to wait until you are on your deathbed to "get right with God." But you might never get the chance. No one knows when, or under what circumstances, their life might be required of them. Suddenly, you will be standing before God, and when He asks that all-important question, "Why should I let you enter into Heaven?" you must have the only answer that will work:

"Because I know Jesus. He died to pay for my sins. He shed His blood so that my sins could be washed away. He is my Savior. Ask Him, He will know me!"

The Cure For Sin

God provided the antidote for your sin, you must receive the cure. Don't wait until it is too late and risk spending eternity in hell.

The Apostle Paul wrote:

> For he says, "In the time of my favor I heard you, and in the day of salvation I helped you." I tell you, now is the time of God's favor, now is the day of salvation.

> — 2 Corinthians 6:2b (NIV)

Now is the day of salvation. It is not a matter of going to this or that church. When I pray for people to come to Christ, I never pray that they will come to my church, though it would be terrific if they did. I say, "Lord, I do not care if they go to a Bible-believing Baptist church, a Bible-believing Methodist church, or a Bible-believing Nazarene church. I do not care who leads them to Jesus because it is so urgent that they come into the kingdom now."

It's Not Too Late

It is not too late for you. Receive Jesus Christ, and live in His love and grace, now and forever. When you die, you will see the gates of Heaven open before you. You will hear the angel chorus singing for joy. Best of all, Jesus will be there to welcome you home! You will be ready for eternity.

Chapter Eight:

Knowing For Sure

Being born again into the Kingdom of God is the single most glorious thing that can happen to a person, but often there are doubts. How do you know for certain that you have been born again? God shows us.

■ *Know-for-sure Test Number One: We know by trusting God's Word, the Bible.*

God's Word is God's integrity. It is an insult not to believe someone's word. God's Word says, "whoever comes to me I will never drive away," (John 6:37b). In Romans 4:5 we are told that God justifies the ungodly. That means we can go to Heaven by nothing we have done, but only by trusting God for what He has done for us. Romans 10:9 tells us that if we confess with our mouth and believe in our heart that God raised Jesus from the dead, we will be saved.

Feelings are not dependable. If you feel like Jesus died on the cross for you, He did. If you do not feel like Jesus died on the cross for you, He still did. I have often said that the first biggest liar in the universe is the Devil, and the second biggest liar is our feelings.

Once I was on a trip with my family. I felt we were on the right road, heading in the right direction, but when we ended up on a little-used, treacherous mountain road I finally consulted the map. We were miles off track! I had made a wrong turn, but at the time it felt right.

Just like that map, the only dependable source of spiritual truth is the Bible, God's Word. Trust it!

■ *Know-for-sure Test Number Two: The Spirit of God bears witness.*

> **The Spirit himself testifies with our spirit that we are God's children.**
>
> **— Romans 8:16**

God's Word and the witness of the Holy Spirit will always agree. But how does the Spirit of God bear witness? It is simple. There will be a new joy and peace in your life (Romans 14:17). You find yourself thinking about Jesus and spiritual things (John 14:26-27, 16:13-14). Daily troubles will no longer upset you as much as they once did. You will experience an inner peace that people will notice. The Holy Spirit will talk to you in your heart.

David Grant, a missionary in India, was exhausted after holding crusades in one city. He decided to take two days off, stay in the city before he had to be in Madras, India for another crusade. So he made arrangements to stay at a friend's house.

He got up very early that first morning, and there was a nagging feeling on the inside urging him to go to Madras immediately.

So he woke up the friend and said, "You have got to take me to the airport. I must get to Madras this morning."

And the friend said, "Why?"

He said, "I don't know. There is just this inner witness telling me I have got to get to Madras."

So the friend got up, got dressed, cleaned up, took him to the airport, and David Grant got an early plane to Madras. He checked into his hotel a day early.

The next night, the hotel clerk met him as he came into the hotel and said, "Mr. Grant. Why did you come in a day early?"

Grant said, "To tell you the truth, I don't know. Nothing really happened here."

The hotel clerk said, "Did you read the paper?" David picked up the paper. The airplane that he was supposed to come in on crashed in the mountains, and there were no survivors. That was why he had the witness of the Holy Spirit telling him to get to Madras one day early, because God knew what was going to happen.

That witness of the Holy Spirit is something we can learn to listen to and obey.

■ *Know-for-sure Test Number Three: A change in your life.*

> Therefore, if anyone is in Christ, he is a new creation; the old has gone, the new has come!
>
> — 2 Corinthians 5:17

Your desires will change. You will want to please God and to learn more about Jesus — in fact you may desire to spend a lot of time at church. Your passion will be to serve the Lord and live your life according to His plan for you.

When you are saved you will want to turn away from sin. You will know that without holiness you will not see God (Hebrews 12:14).

Maybe at one time you developed your own personal form of religion from bits and pieces of philosophies that seemed good to you. But when you are really saved, you will only want to believe what God instructs us to believe.

There is a difference between being spiritually awakened and actually being born again. A spiritually awakened person may be interested in church and "spirituality," but that does not mean that there will necessarily be a change in how he lives his life. In Matthew 18:3, Jesus said we must be converted. That means your old sinful heart does not just get a fresh coat of paint so it looks new. You get a new heart, a changed heart — a heart that yearns for Jesus.

- Your nature will change from longing for sin to longing to be more like Him.

- You will cringe when someone uses the Lord's name as a swear word.

- You will not be perfect. You may stumble from time to time, but you will look back and realize that you have come a long way!

■ *Know-for-sure Test Number Four: Love for other Christians.*

> We know that we have passed from death to life, because we love our brothers. Anyone who does not love remains in death.
>
> — 1 John 3:14

You will find that your choice of friends begins to change. You enjoy a different crowd now.

You will be surprised to find that the company of Christians is enjoyable. Before they seemed like a boring bunch of "holy rollers," but now you love their company. The desire to spend time with Christians is a sign you are on the road to Heaven.

■ *Know-for-sure Test Number Five: There is a battle.*

Think about it: The devil never told you that you were not saved until you became saved. When you were an unredeemed sinner, Satan had nothing to worry about, and he certainly never told you that you were not saved, but once God takes up residence in your heart the devil tries to attack your faith head-on.

Just remember, when doubts assail your mind, it is the last gasp of hell trying to win you back. Demons want to plant doubt in your mind. They want you to feel unworthy of eternal life with God.

> For our struggle is not against flesh and blood, but against the rulers, against the authorities, against the powers of this dark world and against the spiritual forces of evil in the heavenly realms.
>
> — Ephesians 6:12

The good news is Jesus destroyed the works of the devil when He went to the cross.

> He who does what is sinful is of the devil, because the devil has been sinning from the be-

ginning. **The reason the Son of God appeared**
was to destroy the devil's work.

— 1 John 3:8

As you mature as a Christian, you will find that
by using the Name of Jesus, through the power of
the Holy Spirit, you will have complete victory over
the lies of the devil. If the devil tells you that you are
not going to Heaven, rejoice! It is another indication
that you are on the road to Heaven.

"Nobody gets to Heaven just by hearing the Gospel message, but by doing the will of God."

Chapter Nine:

Getting Ready For Heaven

If you were going on a trip, or buying a house, or getting married, you would spend a lot of time working out the details of your plans. The same should be true of our salvation, which is the most important fact about us.

What can we do to prepare for the world beyond?

■ *Checklist Item Number One: Come to Jesus Christ.*

There is no cleansing of sin apart from Him. We can only be made righteous by the blood of the Lamb. We become citizens of Heaven by the new birth. Jesus said:

> I tell you the truth, no one can see the kingdom of God unless he is born again.
>
> — John 3:3

■ *Checklist Item Number Two: Lay up treasures in Heaven now.*

Luke 12:31-34 talks about prayer treasures. Your prayers will go on being answered after you leave this life. Jesus said where your treasure is that is where your heart is going to be. If the bulk of your treasure is here on earth that is where your heart is going to be. If the bulk of your treasure is in Heaven, you have laid up treasures in Heaven, that is where your heart is going to be.

Betty Maltz, a precious Christian, was clinically dead. She told how Jesus showed her around Heaven. One of the things that struck me about her testimony was that Jesus showed her little closets. He opened one of them up and there were ashes on the floor. Betty asked, "What are those?" He said, "This represents the prayers you prayed when you were on earth." Then He took her to someone else's closet and it was filled with ashes. Jesus said, "This person prayed a lot." The Bible says the prayers of the saints go forth like incense.

Lay up for yourselves treasures in Heaven where moth and rust, inflation and deflation, will not corrupt. It will always be there.

■ *Checklist Item Number Three: Do the will of God.*

Nobody gets to Heaven just by hearing the Gospel message, but by *doing* the will of God.

Imagine a man who attends a seminar on how to make lots of money in the stock market, and he listens and says, "Yes, that sounds right to me. What a great plan." But when he goes home he does nothing to move his money from a bank account to the stocks he heard about, and when the stocks start to yield high returns the man has gained nothing. Nevertheless, he believes he should reap the rewards. "After all," he says, "I attended that seminar and heard about the plan. I even agreed with it and thought it would work." But because he never took action, he cannot expect a reward.

Doing the will of God is like investing in the kingdom of Heaven. Jesus said:

> Not everyone who says to me, 'Lord, Lord,' will enter the kingdom of heaven, but only he who does the will of my Father who is in Heaven.
>
> — Matthew 7:21

■ *Checklist Item Number Four: Remember, others are cheering you on.*

> Therefore, since we are surrounded by such a great cloud of witnesses, let us throw off everything that hinders and the sin that so easily

> entangles, and let us run with perseverance the race marked out for us.

> — Hebrews 12:1

There are grandstands in Heaven, just as if we were track runners and our departed friends and family were cheering us to win the race.

■ *Checklist Item Number Five: Remember your biography.*

Remember to make decisions in light of the fact that you are just a visitor here on earth, and a biography is being written about you in Heaven.

> Why, you do not even know what will happen tomorrow. What is your life? You are a mist that appears for a little while and then vanishes.

> — James 4:14

■ *Checklist Item Number Six: Take Jesus into account for everything you think, say and do.*

> Apart from me you can do nothing.

> — John 14:5b

Dr. Irving Harrison, who died and came back to life, made an interesting observation. He said that everyone who has had one of those encounters says the same thing: Once you leave time, it seems like nothing matters anymore, except Jesus. When you stand on the brink of life and death and see yourself moving from time to eternity, you realize that nothing else matters, and that there is nothing except Jesus.

■ *Checklist Item Number Seven: Set your earthly priorities based on Heavenly principles.*

A man on a Navy ship fell overboard, and in the cold ocean currents he began struggling for his life, his lungs filling with water. His shipmates saw him and sent down a lifeboat to rescue him, and when they dragged him up to the deck of the ship, his fellow sailors stood around and made bets as to what the first words out of his mouth would be. Some said they would be curses to God, some said praises. All the while the half-drowned sailor made wild gestures with his hands to communicate something to them. They finally got the water out of his lungs and he gasped and said, "My buddy fell over with me! We gotta get him!"

When he was rescued, his first concern was his friend who was still in danger of drowning. As believers, our number one concern as it relates to other people is getting them into the kingdom before it is too late.

"There will be a day when life ends for each of us, and we will suddenly be somewhere else, either Heaven or hell."

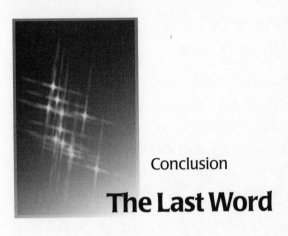

Conclusion

The Last Word

I hope this book has whetted your appetite for Heaven, and given you an idea of what it will be like. Every person alive will visit the world beyond, some bound for Heaven and some for hell.

You and I can hardly imagine what awaits us at the end of our journey if we have given our lives to Jesus Christ as I am sure by now that you have. There will be no earthly moment to match the one when Jesus says to us personally, *"Well done, good and faithful servant. Enter into your Father's rest."*

God is so good! When we live on earth, we live under His grace; His mercies are new every morning. We can say yes or no to Him. But there will be a day when life ends for each of us, and we will suddenly be somewhere else, Heaven or hell. The choice is yours and mine — for now.

How To Become Fit For Heaven And Get A New Start In Life - Now

Have you ever wished you could start your life over again? If so, I have good news for you. Jesus, God's Son, made a way for you to experience a brand new life. Yes, you can start over, regardless of how many wrongs you've done or how "messed up" you may feel right now.

Jesus died on the cross 2000 years ago so that men and women, boys and girls of all ages may be forgiven. Right now, at this very moment, Jesus forgives you of all the wrong you've ever done. But in order to experience that forgiveness and receive a brand new life, you must accept Christ as your Savior. He is mankind's only hope. We can't save ourselves from the guilt, pain, and consequences of sin. So Jesus did it for us.

Nobody can be fit for Heaven apart from accepting Christ, not even the most moral and religious person in the world. Jesus Himself said that nobody will ever get to God unless he comes through Jesus. He said:

> I am the way, the truth, and the life: no man cometh unto the Father, but by me."
>
> —John 14:6

And Saint Paul put it this way:

> For there is one God, and one mediator between God and men, the man Christ Jesus.
>
> —1 Timothy 2:5

And so it's true! There's only one way to experience forgiveness and receive a new start in life. It's through the Lord Jesus Christ. And wow! He is waiting to work miracles in your life because He loves you, no matter what condition you're in right now. He doesn't say, "Clean up your act and I'll accept you!" Instead He says, "Come to Me now, just the way you are, and I'll give you a new life!"

> Therefore if any man be in Christ, he is a new creature: old things are passed away; behold, all things are become new.
>
> —2 Corinthians 5:17

Can you believe it? No strings attached. God's forgiveness, acceptance, and power is available to you right now, just for the asking. God has done His part to give you a new life and some day a home in Heaven — the world beyond. Now, it's up to you.

• Come to Jesus as you are (Romans 3:23).

• Admit your helplessness to save yourself (Romans 6:23, Luke 18:13).

• Ask Jesus to be your Savior and to give you a new start (2 Corinthians 5:17).

•Confess with your mouth that He is Lord (Romans 10:9).

•By faith receive Christ into your life (John 1: 11, 12).

The burden of sin will be quickly rolled away if you do these things. God is standing by you right now to hear you pray. He's ready to send Jesus into your life and is calling the angels together for a celebration in Heaven - a celebration over YOU!

> ...joy shall be in heaven over one sinner that repenteth, more than over ninety and nine just persons, which need no repentance.
>
> —Luke 15:7

If you have never taken this step, why not pray this prayer right now? It will help lead you to a brand new life on this earth, and in Heaven later on. It's what I call a simple prayer of salvation:

> Dear God,
>
> I come to you in the Name of Jesus. Your Word says in John 6:37 that if I turn to You, You will in no way cast me out, but You will take me in just as I am. I thank You, God, for that.
>
> You also said in Romans 10:13 that if I call upon You, I'll be saved. I'm calling on You, Lord, so I know You have now saved me.
>
> I believe Your Son Jesus died on the cross for me, and that He was raised from the dead. I now confess Him as my Lord.

I now have a new life. My sins are gone, and I have a new start, beginning NOW!

Thank You, Lord!

Amen

Congratulations! If you just prayed that prayer for the first time, I want you to call someone. Tell them that you have just made Jesus Christ Lord over your life. You can call the Global Prayer Center at Mount Hope Church in Lansing, Michigan. The phone number is (517) 327-PRAY. I would love to hear from you. You may also contact me on the world wide web at: www.mounthopechurch.org.

Call our toll-free bookstore order line (1-800-888-7284) for your free copy of my book, *The New Life...The Start Of Something Wonderful*. It will help propel you to success in your new life in Christ.

I'll look forward to meeting you one day in the world beyond.

About The Author

Dave Williams is pastor of Mount Hope Church and International Outreach Ministries, with world headquarters in Lansing, Michigan. He has served for over 20 years, leading the church in Lansing from 226 to over 4000 today. Dave sends trained ministers into unreached cities to establish disciple-making churches, and, as a result, today has "branch" churches in the United States, Philippines, and in Africa.

Dave is the founder and president of Mount Hope Bible Training Institute, a fully accredited institute for training ministers and lay people for the work of the ministry. He has authored 45 books including the fifteen-time best seller, *The Start of Something Wonderful* (with over 2,000,000 books sold), and more recently, *The Miracle Results of Fasting*, and *The Road To Radical Riches*.

The Pacesetter's Path telecast is Dave's weekly television program seen over a syndicated network of secular stations, and nationally over the Sky Angel satellite system. Dave has produced over 125 audio cassette programs including the nationally acclaimed School of Pacesetting Leadership which is being used as a training program in churches around the United States, and in Bible Schools in South Africa and the Philippines. He is a popular speaker at conferences, seminars, and conventions. His speaking ministry has taken him across America, Africa, Europe, Asia, and other parts of the world.

Along with his wife, Mary Jo, Dave established The Dave and Mary Jo Williams Charitable Mission (Strategic Global Mission), a mission's ministry for providing scholarships to pioneer pastors and grants to inner-city children's ministries.

Dave's articles and reviews have appeared in national magazines such as Advance, The Pentecostal Evangel, Ministries Today, The Lansing Magazine, The Detroit Free Press and others. Dave, as a private pilot, flies for fun. He is married, has two grown children, and lives in Delta Township, Michigan.

You may write to Pastor Dave Williams:

P.O. Box 80825

Lansing, MI 48908-0825

Please include your special prayer requests when you write, or you may call the Mount Hope Global Prayer Center anytime: (517) 327-PRAY

DECAPOLIS PUBLISHING

For a catalog of products, call:

1-517-321-2780 or

1-800-888-7284

or visit us on the web at:

www.mounthopechurch.org

For Your Spiritual Growth

Here's the help you need for your spiritual journey. These books will encourage you, and give you guidance as you seek to draw close to Jesus and learn of Him. Prepare yourself for fantastic growth!

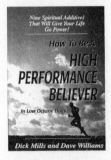

HOW TO BE A HIGH PERFORMANCE BELIEVER
Pour in the nine spiritual additives for real power in your Christian life.

SECRET OF POWER WITH GOD
Tap into the real power with God; the power of prayer. It will change your life!

THE NEW LIFE...
You can get off to a great start on your exciting life with Jesus! Prepare for something wonderful.

MIRACLE RESULTS OF FASTING
You can receive MIRACLE benefits, spiritually and physically, with this practical Christian discipline.

WHAT TO DO IF YOU MISS THE RAPTURE
If you miss the Rapture, there may still be hope, but you need to follow these clear survival tactics.

THE AIDS PLAGUE
Is there hope? Yes, but only Jesus can bring a total and lasting cure to AIDS.

These and other books available from Dave Williams and:

DECAPOLIS PUBLISHING

For Your Spiritual Growth

Here's the help you need for your spiritual journey. These books will encourage you, and give you guidance as you seek to draw close to Jesus and learn of Him. Prepare yourself for fantastic growth!

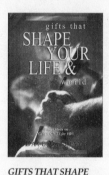

THE ART OF PACESETTING LEADERSHIP
You can become a successful leader with this proven leadership development course.

GIFTS THAT SHAPE YOUR LIFE
Learn which ministry best fits you, and discover your God-given personality gifts, as well as the gifts of others.

GROWING UP IN OUR FATHER'S FAMILY
You can have a family relationship with your heavenly father. Learn how God cares for you.

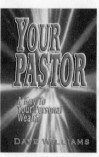

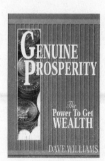

SUPERNATURAL SOULWINNING
How will we reach our family, friends, and neighbors in this short time before Christ's return?

YOUR PASTOR: A KEY TO YOUR PERSONAL WEALTH
By honoring your pastor you can actually be setting yourself up for a financial blessing from God!

GENUINE PROSPERITY
Learn what it means to be truly prosperous! God gives us the power to get wealth!

These and other books available from Dave Williams and:

DECAPOLIS PUBLISHING

For Your Spiritual Growth

Here's the help you need for your spiritual journey. These books will encourage you, and give you guidance as you seek to draw close to Jesus and learn of Him. Prepare yourself for fantastic growth!

SOMEBODY OUT THERE NEEDS YOU
Along with the gift of salvation comes the great privilege of spreading the gospel of Jesus Christ.

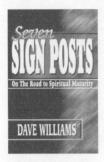

SEVEN SIGNPOSTS TO SPIRITUAL MATURITY
Examine your life to see where you are on the road to spiritual maturity.

THE PASTORS PAY
How much is your pastor worth? Who should set his pay? Discover the scriptural guidelines for paying your pastor.

DECEPTION, DELUSION & DESTRUCTION
Recognize spiritual deception and unmask spiritual blindness.

THE ROAD TO RADICAL RICHES
Are you ready to jump from "barely getting by" to Gods plan for putting you on the road to Radical Riches?

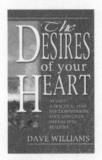

THE DESIRES OF YOUR HEART
Yes, Jesus wants to give you the desires of your heart, and make them realities.

For Your Successful Life

These video cassettes will give you successful principles to apply to your whole life. Each a different topic, and each a fantastic teaching of how living by God's Word can give you total success!

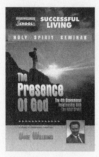

THE PRESENCE OF GOD
Find out how you can have a more dynamic relationship with the Holy Spirit.

FILLED WITH THE HOLY SPIRIT
You can rejoice and share with others in this wonderful experience of God.

GIFTS THAT CHANGE YOUR WORLD
Learn which ministry best fits you, and discover your God-given personality gifts, as well as the gifts of others.

THE SCHOOL OF PACESETTING LEADERSHIP
Leaders are made, not born. You can become a successful leader with this proven leadership development course.

MIRACLE RESULTS OF FASTING
Fasting is your secret weapon in spiritual warfare. Learn how you'll benefit spiritually and physically! Six video messages.

A SPECIAL LADY
If you feel used and abused, this video will show you how you really are in the eyes of Jesus. You are special!

These and other videos available from Dave Williams and:

DECAPOLIS PUBLISHING

For Your Successful Life

These video cassettes will give you successful principles to apply to your whole life. Each a different topic, and each a fantastic teaching of how living by God's Word can give you total success!

HOW TO BE A HIGH PERFORMANCE BELIEVER
Pour in the nine spiritual additives for real power in your Christian life.

THE UGLY WORMS OF JUDGMENT
Recognizing the decay of judgment in your life is your first step back into God's fullness.

WHAT TO DO WHEN YOU FEEL WEAK AND DEFEATED
Learn about God's plan to bring you out of defeat and into His principles of victory!

WHY SOME ARE NOT HEALED
Discover the obstacles that hold people back from receiving their miracle and how God can help them receive the very best!

BREAKING THE POWER OF POVERTY
The principality of mammon will try to keep you in poverty. Put God FIRST and watch Him bring you into a wealthy place.

HERBS FOR HEALTH
A look at the concerns and fears of modern medicine. Learn the correct ways to open the doors to your healing.

These and other videos available from Dave Williams and:

DECAPOLIS PUBLISHING

Running Your Race

These simple but powerful audio cassette singles will help give you the edge you need. Run your race to win!

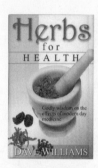

LONELY IN THE MIDST OF A CROWD
Loneliness is a devastating disease. Learn how to trust and count on others to help.

HERBS FOR HEALTH
A look at the concerns and fears of modern medicine. Learn the correct ways to open the doors to your healing.

HOW TO GET ANYTHING YOU WANT
You can learn the way to get anything you want from God!

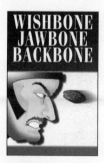

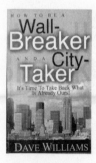

WISHBONE, JAWBONE, BACKBONE
Learn about King David, and how his three "bones" for success can help you in your life quest.

FATAL ENTICEMENTS
Learn how you can avoid the vice-like grip of sin and it's fatal enticements that hold people captive.

HOW TO BE A WALL BREAKER AND A CITY TAKER
You can be a powerful force for advancing the Kingdom of Jesus Christ!

These and other audio tapes available from Dave Williams and:

DECAPOLIS PUBLISHING

Expanding Your Faith

These exciting audio teaching series will help you to grow and mature in your walk with Christ. Get ready for amazing new adventures in faith!

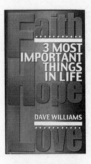

WHY DO SOME SUFFER
Find out why some people seem to have suffering in their lives, and find out how to avoid it in your life.

SIN'S GRIP
Learn how you can avoid the vice-like grip of sin and it's fatal enticements that hold people captive.

FAITH, HOPE, & LOVE
Listen and let these three "most important things in life" change you.

PSALM 91
THE PROMISE OF PROTECTION
Everyone is looking for protection in these perilous times. God promises protection for those who rest in Him.

DEVELOPING
THE SPIRIT OF A CONQUEROR
You can be a conqueror through Christ! Also, find out how to *keep* those things that you have conquered.

YOUR SPECTACULAR MIND
Identify wrong thinking and negative influences in your life.

These and other audio tapes available from Dave Williams and:

DECAPOLIS PUBLISHING

Expanding Your Faith

These exciting audio teaching series will help you to grow and mature in your walk with Christ. Get ready for amazing new adventures in faith!

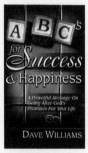

ABCs OF SUCCESS AND HAPPINESS
Learn how to go after God's promises for your life. Happiness and success can be yours today!

FORGIVENESS
The miracle remedy for many of life's problems is found in this basic key for living.

UNTANGLING YOUR TROUBLES
You can be a "trouble untangler" with the help of Jesus!

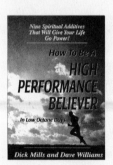

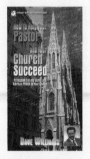

HOW TO BE A HIGH PERFORMANCE BELIEVER
Put in the nine spiritual additives to help run your race and get the prize!

BEING A DISCIPLE AND MAKING DISCIPLES
You can learn to be a "disciple maker" to almost anyone.

HOW TO HELP YOUR PASTOR & CHURCH SUCCEED
You can be an integral part of your church's & pastor's success.

These and other audio tapes available from Dave Williams and:

DECAPOLIS
PUBLISHING

More Products by Dave Williams

BOOK Title	Price
The New Life — The Start Of Something Wonderful	$1.95
End Times Bible Prophecy	$4.95
Seven Sign Posts On the Road To Spiritual Maturity	$4.95
Somebody Out There Needs You	$4.95
Growing Up In Our Father's Family	$4.95
Grief & Mourning	$7.95
The World Beyond — Mysteries Of Heaven	$7.95
The Secret Of Power With God	$7.95
What To Do If You Miss the Rapture	$9.95
Genuine Prosperity	$9.95
The Miracle Results Of Fasting	$9.95
How To Be A High Performance Believer	$9.95
Gifts That Shape Your Life & Change Your World	$10.95
Road To Radical Riches	$19.95

CD Title	Num. of CDs	Price
Middle East Crisis	1	$12.00
Setting Our Houses In Order	1	$12.00
Too Much Baggage?	1	$12.00
Jesus Loves Sinners	1	$12.00
How To Get Your Breakthrough	1	$12.00
Amazing Power Of Desire	1	$12.00
Wounded Spirit	1	$12.00
The Attack On America (Sept. 11, 2001)	1	$12.00
Radical Wealth	5	$60.00

VIDEO Title	Num. of Videos	Price
What To Do When You Are Going Through Hell	1	$19.95
Acres Of Diamonds — The Valley Of Baca	1	$19.95
120 Elite Warriors	1	$19.95
What To Do If You Miss the Rapture	1	$19.95
Regaining Your Spiritual Momentum	1	$19.95
Herbs For Health	1	$19.95
TheDestructive Power Of Legalism	1	$19.95
4 Ugly Worms Of Judgment	1	$19.95
Grief and Mourning	1	$19.95
Breaking the Power Of Poverty	1	$19.95
Triple Benefits Of Fasting	1	$19.95
Why Some Are Not Healed	2	$39.95
Miracle Results Of Fasting	3	$59.95
ABCs Of Success and Happiness	3	$59.95
Gifts That Shape Your Life and Change Your World	5	$99.95

AUDIO Title	Num. of Tapes	Price
Lonely In the Midst Of a Crowd	1	$6.00
How To Get Anything You Want	1	$6.00
Untangling Your Troubles	2	$12.00
Healing Principles In the Ministry Of Jesus	2	$12.00
Acres Of Diamonds — The Valley Of Baca	2	$12.00
Finding Peace	2	$12.00
Criticize & Judge	2	$12.00
Judgment On America	2	$12.00
Triple Benefits Of Fasting	2	$12.00
Global Confusion	2	$12.00
The Cure For a Broken Heart	2	$12.00
Help! I'm Getting Older	2	$12.00
Regaining Your Spiritual Momentum	2	$12.00
The Destructive Power Of Legalism	2	$12.00
Three Most Important Things In Life	3	$18.00
The Final Series	3	$18.00
The Mysteries of Heaven	3	$18.00
Dave Williams' Crash Course In Intercessory Prayer	3	$18.00
Forgiveness — The Miracle Remedy	4	$24.00
How Long Until the End	4	$24.00
What To Do When You Feel Weak and Defeated	4	$24.00
Sin's Grip	4	$24.00
Why Some Are Not Healed	4	$24.00
Bible Cures	4	$24.00
Belial	4	$24.00
God is Closer Than You Think	5	$30.00
Decoding the Apocalypse	5	$30.00
Winning Your Inner Conflict	5	$30.00
Radical Wealth	5	$30.00
Violent Action For Your Wealth	5	$30.00
The Presence Of God	6	$36.00
Your Spectacular Mind	6	$36.00
The Miracle Results of Fasting	6	$36.00
Developing the Spirit Of a Conqueror	6	$36.00
Why Do Some Suffer	6	$36.00
Overcoming Life's Adversities	6	$36.00
Faith Steps	6	$36.00
ABCs For Success & Happiness	6	$36.00
The Best Of Dave Williams	6	$36.00
How To Help Your Pastor & Church Succeed	8	$48.00
Being a Disciple & Making Disciples	8	$48.00
High Performance Believer	8	$48.00
True Or False	8	$48.00
The End Times	8	$48.00
The Beatitudes — Success 101	8	$48.00
Hearing the Voice Of God	10	$60.00
Gifts That Shape Your Life — Personality Gifts	10	$60.00
Gifts That Shape Your Life & Change Your World — Ministry Gifts	10	$60.00
Daniel Parts 1 & 2 (Both parts 6 tapes each)	12	$72.00
Roadblocks To Your Radical Wealth	12	$72.00
Revelation Parts 1 & 2 (part 1 - 6 tapes; part 2 - 8 tapes)	14	$84.00

Mount Hope Ministries

Mount Hope Missions & International Outreach
Care Ministries, Deaf Ministries
& Support Groups
Access to Christ for the Physically Impaired
Community Outreach Ministries
Mount Hope Youth Ministries
Mount Hope Bible Training Institute
The Hope Store and Decapolis Publishing
The Pacesetter's Path Telecast
The Pastor's Minute Radio Broadcast
Mount Hope Children's Ministry
Champions Club and Sidewalk Sunday School
The Saturday Care Clinic

When you're facing a struggle and need someone to pray with you, please call us at (517) 321-CARE or (517) 327-PRAY. We have pastors on duty 24 hours a day. We know you hurt sometimes and need a pastor, a minister, or a prayer partner. There will be ministers and prayer partners here for you.

If you'd like to write, we'd be honored to pray for you. Our address is:

MOUNT HOPE CHURCH
202 S. CREYTS RD.
LANSING, MI 48917
(517) 321-CARE or (517) 321-2780
FAX (517)321-6332
TDD (517) 321-8200

www.mounthopechurch.org

email: mhc@mounthopechurch.org

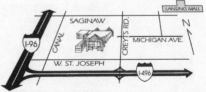

West of the Lansing Mall, on Creyts at Michigan Ave.